Tree Town

Hawys Morgan

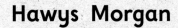

OXFORD
UNIVERSITY PRESS

OXFORD
UNIVERSITY PRESS

Great Clarendon Street, Oxford, OX2 6DP, United Kingdom

Oxford University Press is a department of the University of Oxford. It furthers the University's objective of excellence in research, scholarship, and education by publishing worldwide. Oxford is a registered trade mark of Oxford University Press in the UK and in certain other countries

Text © Hawys Morgan 2016

Illustrations © Frann Preston-Gannon 2016

Inside cover notes written by Karra McFarlane

British Library Cataloguing in Publication Data
Data available

ISBN: 978-0-19-837102-1

10 9 8

Paper used in the production of this book is a natural, recyclable product made from wood grown in sustainable forests. The manufacturing process conforms to the environmental regulations of the country of origin.

Printed in China

Acknowledgements

Series Editor: Nikki Gamble

All photography by Shutterstock

Contents

Tree Roots

den

fox cub

roots

Tree roots are strong. Roots can drink from the wet soil.

The fox digs a den in the roots.

Fox

Lives in: roots
Food: plants, animals, insects

Tree Trunk

moss

The trunk has hard bark on it.

fungus

Earwig

Lives in: bark, logs, leaves

Food: insects, plants

six legs →

I will put the earwig back on the tree!

Leaves

caterpillar

eggs

Look at the caterpillar
eggs on the leaf.

Catkins

moth

catkin

Catkins are flowers on a tree.

Moth

Lives in: tree
Food: nectar

wings

six legs

catkin

The moth's wings are soft and thin. My hands might hurt it so I have a net.

Nest

treecreeper

chicks

nest

twigs

moss

Treecreepers nest in the bark.
They look for food in the tree
for the chicks.

Treecreeper

Lives in: trees
Food: nuts, seeds, insects

13

Tree Town

leaves

treetop

What can you see in a tree near you?

Lots of animals and insects live in the tree. It is just like a town for them!

trunk

roots

Glossary

fungus: a living thing, like a plant but with no leaves or flowers, such as a mushroom

nectar: a sweet liquid from flowers

Index